21st Century Junior Library

MAKING A DIFFERENCE WITH THE AMERICAN RED CROSS

Katie Marsico

How Can I Help?

Published in the United States of America by:

CHERRY LAKE PRESS
2395 South Huron Parkway, Suite 200, Ann Arbor, MI 48104
www.cherrylakepress.com

Reading Adviser: Marla Conn, Read With Me Now
Photo Credits: American Red Cross : © Kuosumo/Dreamstime.com, cover, title page; © Seth Perlman/ASSOCIATED PRESS, 5; Andrea Booher/FEMA via Wikimedia Commons, public domain, 6; George Jumara/U.S. Army Corps of Engineers/Flickr.com, 7; Airman Jared Lovett/U.S. Air Force, 8; Greg Henshall/FEMA via Wikimedia Commons, public domain, 9; Courtesy of the National Park Service, Little Bighorn Battlefield National Monument, 11; © Everett Collection/Shutterstock, 12; Library of Congress, Prints & Photographs Division, Farm Security Administration/Office of War Information, 13; © Soros Banjongpian/iStock.com, 14; © AFM Visuals/Shutterstock, 17; © SlavkoSereda/Dreamstime.com, 18; Petty Officer 3rd Class Joshua Nistas/Joint Task Force Guantanamo Public Affairs/DVIDSHUB, 20; © Lina Reshetnyk/Dreamstime.com, 21

Cherry Lake Press is an imprint of Cherry Lake Publishing Group.

Library of Congress Cataloging-in-Publication Data

Names: Marsico, Katie, 1980- author.
Title: Making a difference with the American Red Cross / written byKatie Marsico.
Description: Ann Arbor, MI : Cherry Lake Publishing, [2024] | Series: How can I help? | Audience: Grades 2-3 | Summary: "The American Red Cross's volunteers and staff work year-round to provide disaster relief, run blood drives, and supply medicine and food to those in need. Readers will explore the history and impact of this organization and how it brings communities together in times of crisis"– Provided by publisher.
Identifiers: LCCN 2024010026 | ISBN 9781668946800 (hardcover) | ISBN 9781668948194 (paperback) | ISBN 9781668949719 (ebook) | ISBN 9781668954270 (pdf)
Subjects: LCSH: American Red Cross–History–Juvenile literature. | Disaster relief–Juvenile literature.
Classification: LCC HV568 .M264 2024 | DDC 361.7/634–dc23/eng/20240301
LC record available at https://lccn.loc.gov/2024010026

Cherry Lake Publishing Group would like to acknowledge the work of the Partnership for 21st Century Learning, a Network of Battelle for Kids. Please visit Battelle for Kids online for more information.

Printed in the United States of America

Note from publisher: Websites change regularly, and their future contents are outside of our control. Supervise children when conducting any recommended online searches for extended learning opportunities.

CHERRY LAKE PRESS

CONTENTS

COMFORT IN A COLD WORLD

A December ice storm knocks out power in Decatur, Illinois. It leaves thousands of homes and businesses dark and cold. This is dangerous for people who are old, sick, or caring for small children.

Fortunately, the Red Cross can help. This group serves hot food at local shelters. It helps those who had to leave their homes stay safe and warm until the power returns.

People who need help can go to a Red Cross shelter for a free meal.

Think!

What would life be like if you were without power for more than a few days? Furnaces and air conditioners both use electricity. So do microwaves, televisions, computers, and phones.

Its members help communities struggling with both natural and man-made disasters. They help people affected by storms, floods, fires, earthquakes, and war. The group also encourages communities to grow and develop. It works with residents to improve everything from health care to **sanitation**.

The Red Cross can help rebuild a neighborhood after a storm destroys it.

Make a Guess!

Are you able to guess how many people the Red Cross helps? Think big! It responds to around 60,000 disasters every year. In 2023 alone, it trained 6.9 million people in first aid, resuscitation, and lifeguard certification.

This organization supports programs that respect and include people of all different backgrounds and beliefs. It is firmly against **discrimination** and violence.

The American Red Cross goes wherever people need help, such as this U.S. Army base in Afghanistan.

Look!

With an adult, head to your local library or go online. Look for pictures of the Red Cross. What kind of work do you see volunteers doing? How are they helping in communities around the world?

The Red Cross is interested in helping as many people as possible. They don't favor one group over another. This is true even when two nations or several groups are at war.

FROM 1863 ONWARD

Swiss businessman Henry Dunant developed the first Red Cross. In 1859, Dunant was in Italy. A war was going on there. Dunant gathered local residents together. He called on them to give the soldiers comfort and medical attention.

Afterward, Dunant suggested setting up a national organization. He wanted people to be

Soldiers on all sides of every war need medical treatment.

Think!

Think about why it's helpful for Red Cross societies to be **neutral**. What if they weren't? Do you think it would change how these groups give aid during a war?

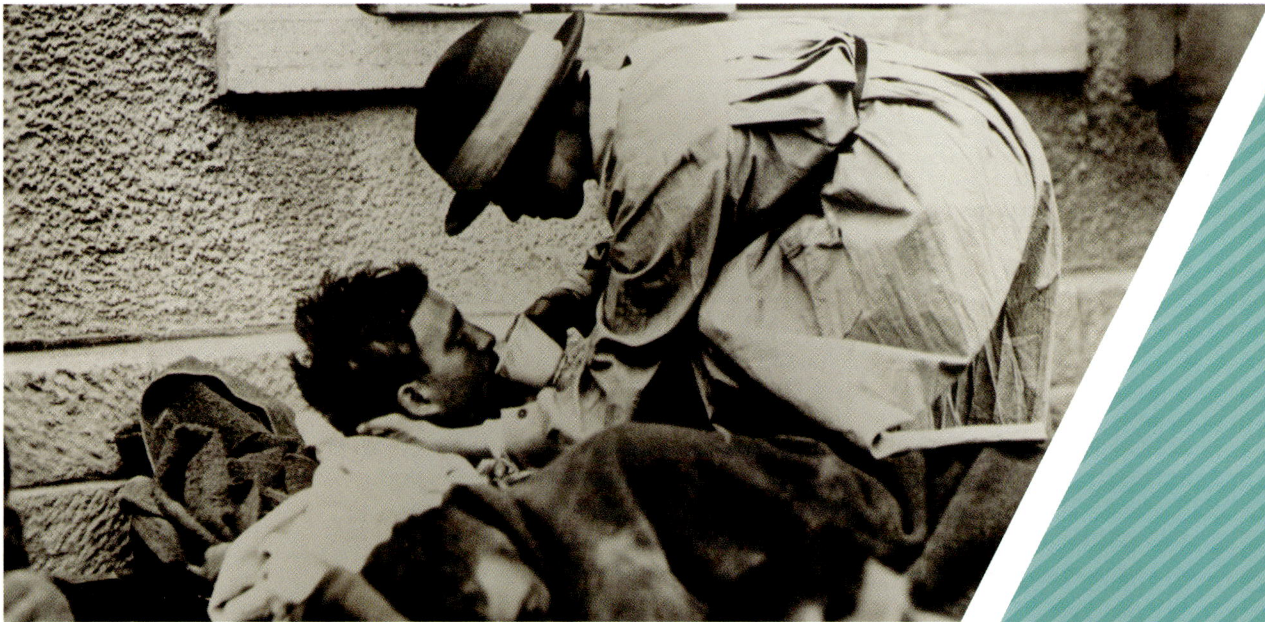

prepared to care for the wounded during a war. Volunteers eventually learned to help communities dealing with natural disasters and **outbreaks** of illness, too.

Dunant's work inspired Clara Barton, an American woman devoted to helping others. In 1881, Barton founded the American Red Cross in Washington, D.C.

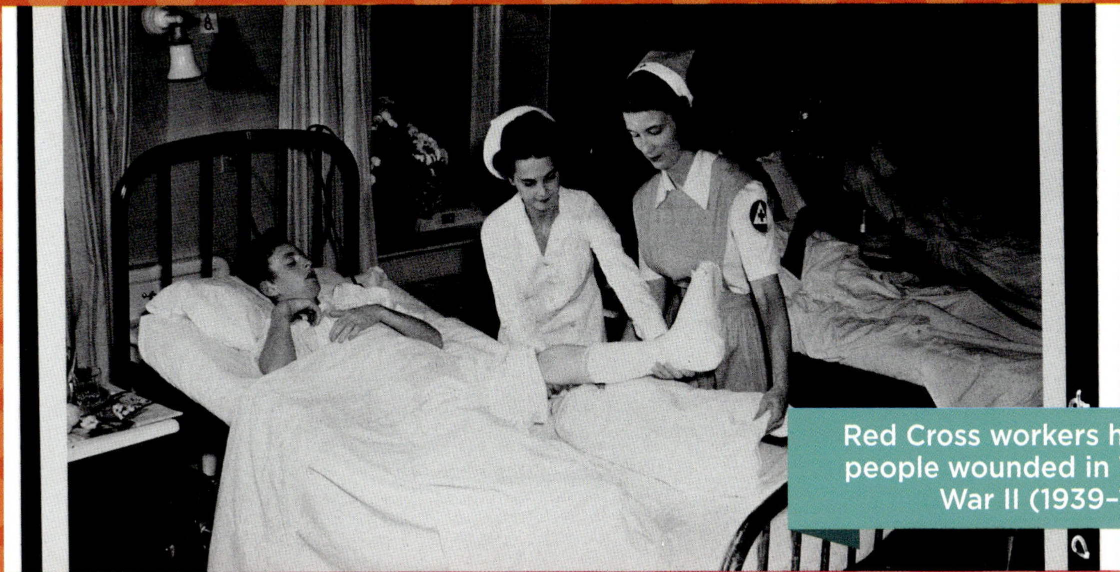

Red Cross workers helped people wounded in World War II (1939–1945).

The American Red Cross is now over 140 years old. It has responded to over three million disasters. It continues Clara Barton's mission to help all those in need.

Look!

This photo shows Red Cross workers in the 1940s. Compare what you see to photos of today's Red Cross workers. What differences do you notice?

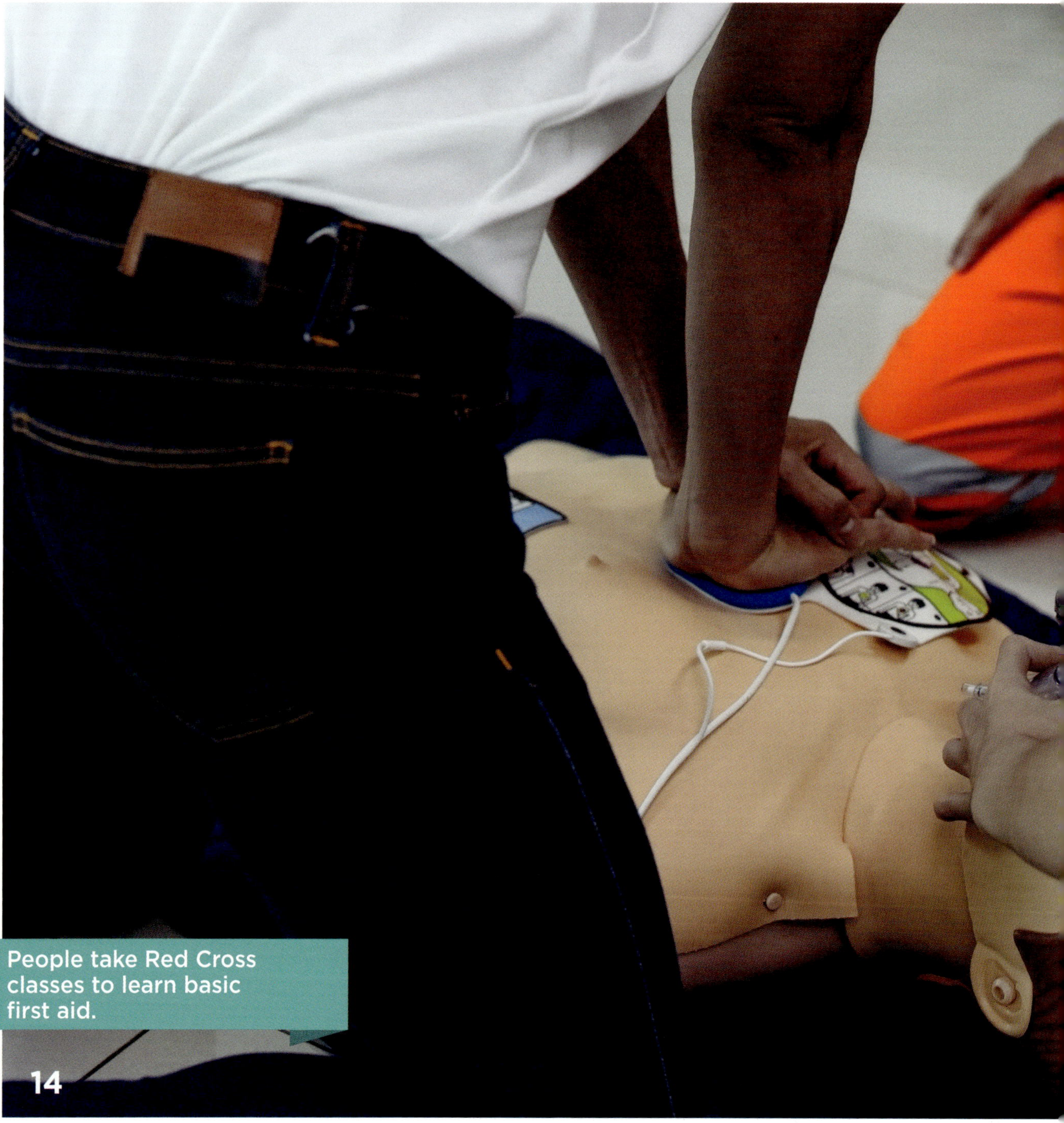

People take Red Cross classes to learn basic first aid.

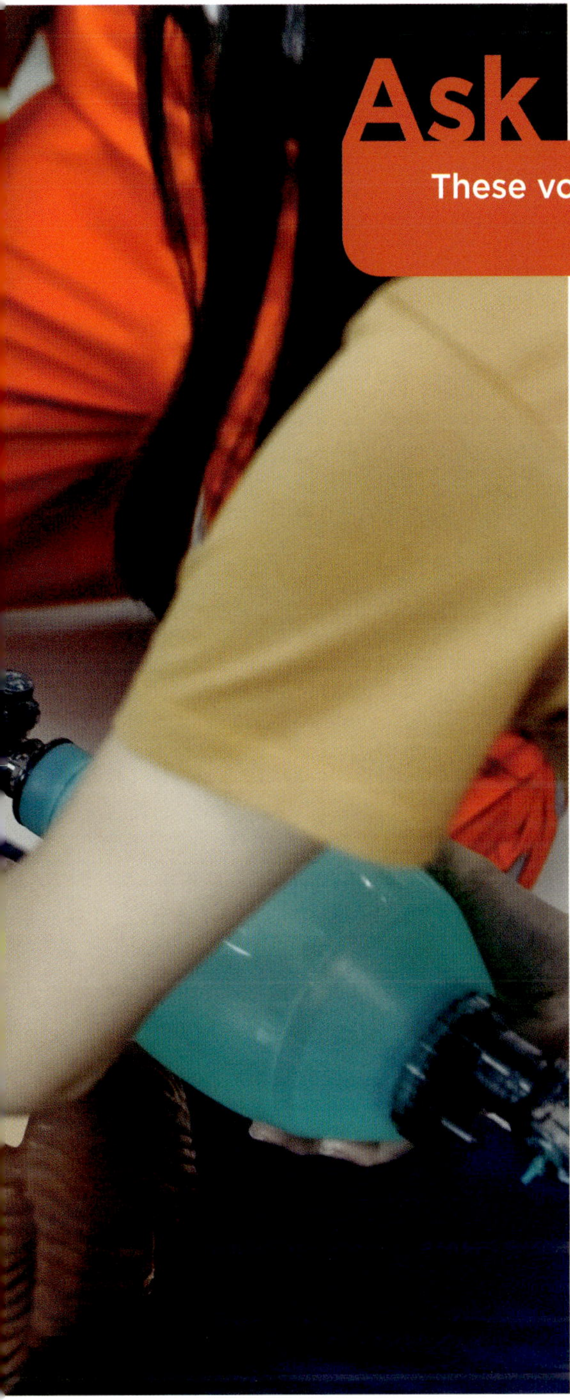

Ask Questions!

These volunteers are practicing CPR. Ask an adult to help you find out what CPR involves.

Today, nearly every nation has a Red Cross organization. Some countries call it the Red Crescent Society.

These organizations mainly depend on the efforts of 14 million volunteers. The volunteers teach first aid, act as **translators**, and provide food and shelter to disaster victims. Around 300,000 volunteers work each year for the American Red Cross alone.

EFFORTS THAT IMPROVE LIVES

There are many ways that the Red Cross helps communities prepare for and deal with disaster. They organize blood drives. They also provide disaster victims with emergency medical treatment and **counseling**.

Volunteers pass out food, fresh water, and **hygiene** kits. They run shelters where people are able to rest and recover indoors. The Red Cross helps victims reunite with friends and family, too.

Blood drives are one way that people can contribute to the work of the Red Cross.

Make a Guess!

A blood drive is an event where people come to donate some blood. Try guessing how a blood drive helps prepare a community for disaster.

The International Federation of Red Cross helped to feed Ukrainians in 2022 in the midst of attacks by Russia.

Ask Questions!

Ask your parents and teachers what projects the American Red Cross and the Canadian Red Cross are currently involved in. These volunteers often help in other countries.

The Red Cross doesn't wait for disaster to strike to build stronger, safer communities. Some volunteers create programs to provide better sanitation and a steady supply of food and fresh water. Others educate the public about **vaccinations** and stopping the spread of disease.

When a disaster strikes a community, the Red Cross will go there as fast as they can.

Society members also hold workshops and community meetings to help end violence and discrimination.

Thanks to the American Red Cross, individuals and entire families are able to recover from disaster.

Create!

Create a list of ways you and your classmates and friends could help to support the Red Cross. Perhaps your school could host a bake sale or yard sale to raise money to help others.

GLOSSARY

counseling (KOWN-suhl-ing) guidance and advice that support emotional health

discrimination (dis-krih-muh-NAY-shuhn) the act of treating a person or group unfairly because of their beliefs, background, or physical differences

hygiene (HYE-jeen) keeping yourself and the things around you clean, in order to stay healthy

neutral (NOO-truhl) impartial or unwilling to take sides in a conflict

outbreaks (OWT-brayks) sudden beginnings of something unpleasant

sanitation (sah-nuh-TAY-shuhn) conditions related to public health

translators (TRANS-layt-uhrz) people who change speech or text into a different language; often to help people communicate

vaccinations (vak-suh-NAY-shuhnz) shots or drops taken by mouth that protect people against various diseases

FIND OUT MORE

Books

Connolly, Sean. *The International Red Cross*. Mankato, MN: Smart Apple Media, 2009.

Hunter, Nick. *Disaster Relief*. Chicago: Heinemann Library, 2012.

Wade, Mary Dodson. *Amazing Civil War Nurse Clara Barton.* Berkeley Heights, NJ: Enslow Publishers, 2010.

Websites

With an adult, find out more online with these suggested searches.

American Red Cross—Mobilizing the Power of Youth

Visit this Web site to find out how kids support the American Red Cross.

Canadian Red Cross—Red Cross Youth

Review this Web page for videos and stories about how kids share their time and effort with the Canadian Red Cross.

INDEX

ABOUT THE AUTHOR

Katie Marsico is the author of more than 150 children's books. She lives in a suburb of Chicago, Illinois, with her husband and children.